'... in this painting of Leonardo's there was a smile so pleasing that it seemed divine rather than human ...'

GIORGIO VASARI
Born 1511, Arezzo, Italy
Died 1574, Florence, Italy

This selection of biographies published in its original Italian
in 1550. They are taken from *Lives of the Artists (Volume I)*,
Penguin Classics, 1987.

VASARI IN PENGUIN CLASSICS
Lives of the Artists (Volume I)
Lives of the Artists (Volume II)

GIORGIO VASARI

Leonardo da Vinci

Translated by
George Bull

PENGUIN BOOKS

PENGUIN CLASSICS

UK | USA | Canada | Ireland | Australia
India | New Zealand | South Africa

Penguin Books is part of the Penguin Random House group of companies
whose addresses can be found at global.penguinrandomhouse.com.

Penguin
Random House
UK

This selection published in Penguin Classics 2015
002

Translation copyright © George Bull, 1965

The moral right of the translator has been asserted

Set in 9.5/13 pt Baskerville 10 Pro
Typeset by Jouve (UK), Milton Keynes
Printed in Great Britain by Clays Ltd, St Ives plc

Contents

Life of Leonardo da Vinci   1

Life of Fra Filippo Lippi   26

Life of Sandro Botticelli   40

Life of Leonardo da Vinci

FLORENTINE PAINTER AND
SCULPTOR, 1452–1519

In the normal course of events many men and women are
born with various remarkable qualities and talents; but
occasionally, in a way that transcends nature, a single
person is marvellously endowed by heaven with beauty,
grace, and talent in such abundance that he leaves other
men far behind, all his actions seem inspired, and indeed
everything he does clearly comes from God rather than
from human art.

Everyone acknowledged that this was true of Leonardo
da Vinci, an artist of outstanding physical beauty who
displayed infinite grace in everything he did and who
cultivated his genius so brilliantly that all problems he
studied he solved with ease. He possessed great strength
and dexterity; he was a man of regal spirit and tremen-
dous breadth of mind; and his name became so famous
that not only was he esteemed during his lifetime but
his reputation endured and became even greater after
his death.

This marvellous and divinely inspired Leonardo was

1

the son of Piero da Vinci. He would have been very proficient at his early lessons if he had not been so volatile and unstable; for he was always setting himself to learn many things only to abandon them almost immediately. Thus he began to learn arithmetic, and after a few months he had made so much progress that he used to baffle his master with the questions and problems that he raised. For a little while he attended to music, and then he very soon resolved to learn to play the lyre, for he was naturally of an elevated and refined disposition; and with this instrument he accompanied his own charming improvised singing. All the same, for all his other enterprises Leonardo never ceased drawing and working in relief, pursuits which best suited his temperament.

Realizing this, and considering the quality of his son's intelligence, Piero one day took some of Leonardo's drawings along to Andrea del Verrocchio (who was a close friend of his) and earnestly begged him to say whether it would be profitable for the boy to study design. Andrea was amazed to see what extraordinary beginnings Leonardo had made and he urged Piero to make him study the subject. So Piero arranged for Leonardo to enter Andrea's workshop. The boy was delighted with this decision, and he began to practise not only one branch of the arts but all the branches in which design plays a part. He was marvellously gifted, and he proved himself to be a first-class geometrician in his work as a sculptor and architect. In his youth Leonardo made in clay several heads of women, with smiling faces, of which plaster casts are still being made, as well as some children's heads executed as if by a mature artist. He also did many architectural drawings both of ground plans and of other elevations, and, while still young, he was the first to propose reducing the Arno to a navigable canal between Pisa and Florence. He made designs for mills, fulling machines, and engines that could be driven by water-power; and as he intended to be a painter by profession he carefully studied drawing from life. Sometimes he made clay models, draping the figures with rags dipped in plaster, and then drawing them painstakingly on fine Rheims cloth or prepared linen. These drawings were done in black and white with the point of the brush, and the results were marvellous, as one can see from the examples I have in my book of drawings. Besides this, Leonardo did beautiful and detailed drawings on paper which are unrivalled for the perfection of their finish. (I have an example of these in a superb head in coloured silverpoint.) Altogether, his genius was so wonderfully inspired by the grace of God, his powers of expression were so powerfully fed by a willing memory and intellect, and his writing conveyed his ideas so precisely, that his arguments and reasonings confounded the most formidable critics. In addition, he used to make models and plans showing how to excavate and tunnel through mountains without difficulty, so as to pass from one level to another; and he demonstrated how to lift and draw great weights by means of levers, hoists, and winches, and ways of cleansing harbours and using pumps to suck up water from great depths. His brain was always busy on such devices, and one can find drawings of his ideas and experiments scattered among our craftsmen today; I myself have seen many of them. He also spent a great deal of time in making a pattern of a series of knots, so arranged that the connecting thread can be traced from one end to the other and the complete design fills a round space. There exists a splendid engraving of one of these fine and intricate designs, with these words in the centre: *Leonardus Vinci Academia.*

Among his models and plans there was one which Leonardo would often put before the citizens who were then governing Florence – many of them men of great discernment – showing how he proposed to raise and place steps under the church of San Giovanni without damaging the fabric. His arguments were so cogent that they would allow themselves to be convinced, although when they all went their several ways each of them would realize the impossibility of what Leonardo suggested.

Leonardo's disposition was so lovable that he commanded everyone's affection. He owned, one might say, nothing and he worked very little, yet he always kept servants as well as horses. These gave him great pleasure as indeed did all the animal creation which he treated with wonderful love and patience. For example, often when he was walking past the places where birds were sold he would pay the price asked, take them from their cages, and let them fly off into the air, giving them back their lost freedom. In return he was so favoured by nature that to whatever he turned his mind or thoughts the results were always inspired and perfect; and his lively and delightful works were incomparably graceful and realistic.

Clearly, it was because of his profound knowledge of painting that Leonardo started so many things without finishing them; for he was convinced that his hands, for all their skill, could never perfectly express the subtle and wonderful ideas of his imagination. Among his many interests was included the study of nature; he investigated the properties of plants and then observed the motion of the heavens, the path of the moon, and the course of the sun.

I mentioned earlier that when he was still young Leonardo entered the workshop of Andrea del Verrocchio. Now at that time Verrocchio was working on a panel picture showing the Baptism of Christ by St John, for which Leonardo painted an angel who was holding some garments; and despite his youth, he executed it in such a manner that his angel was far better than the figures painted by Andrea. This was the reason why Andrea would never touch colours again, he was so ashamed that a boy understood their use better than he did. Leonardo was then commissioned to make a cartoon (for a tapestry to be woven of gold and silk in Flanders and sent to the king of Portugal) showing the sin of Adam and Eve in the Garden of Paradise. For this he drew with the brush in chiaroscuro, with the lights in lead-white, a luxuriant meadow full of different kinds of animals; and it can truthfully be said that for diligence and faithfulness to nature nothing could be more inspired or perfect. There is a fig tree, for example, with its leaves foreshortened and its branches drawn from various aspects, depicted with such loving care that the brain reels at the thought that a man could have such patience. And there is a palm tree, the radiating crown of which is drawn with such marvellous skill that no one without Leonardo's understanding and patience could have done it. The work was not carried any farther and so today the cartoon is still in Florence, in the blessed house of the Magnificent Ottaviano de' Medici to whom it was presented not long ago by Leonardo's uncle.

The story goes that once when Piero da Vinci was at his house in the country one of the peasants on his farm, who had made himself a buckler out of a fig tree that he had cut down, asked him as a favour to have it painted for him in Florence. Piero was very happy to do this, since the man was very adept at snaring birds and fishing and Piero himself very often made use of him in these pursuits. He took the buckler to Florence, and without saying a word about whom it belonged to he asked Leonardo to paint something on it. Some days later Leonardo examined the buckler, and, finding that it was warped, badly made, and clumsy, he straightened it in the fire and then gave it to a turner who, from the rough and clumsy thing that it was, made it smooth and even. Then having given it a coat of gesso and prepared it in his own way Leonardo started to think what he could paint on it so as to terrify anyone who saw it and produce the same effect as the head of Medusa. To do what he wanted Leonardo carried into a room of his own, which no one ever entered except himself, a number of green and other kinds of lizards, crickets, serpents, butterflies, locusts, bats, and various strange creatures of this nature; from all these he took and assembled different parts to create a fearsome and horrible monster which emitted a poisonous breath and turned the air to fire. He depicted the creature emerging from the dark cleft of a rock, belching forth venom from its open throat, fire from its eyes and smoke from its nostrils in so macabre a fashion that the effect was altogether monstrous and horrible. Leonardo took so long over the work that the stench of the dead animals in his room became unbearable, although he himself failed to notice because of his great love of painting. By the time he had finished the painting both the peasant and his father had stopped inquiring after it; but all the same he told his father that he could send for the buckler when convenient, since his work on it was completed. So one morning Piero went along to the room in order to get the buckler, knocked at the door, and was told by Leonardo to wait for a moment. Leonardo went back into the room, put the buckler on an easel in the light, and shaded the window; then he asked Piero to come in and see it. When his eyes fell on it Piero was completely taken by surprise and gave a sudden start, not realizing that he was looking at the buckler and that the form he saw was, in fact, painted on it. As he backed away, Leonardo checked him and said:

'This work certainly serves its purpose. It has produced the right reaction, so now you can take it away.'

Piero thought the painting was indescribably marvellous and he was loud in praise of Leonardo's ingenuity. And then on the quiet he bought from a pedlar another buckler, decorated with a heart pierced by a dart, and he gave this to the peasant, who remained grateful to him for the rest of his days. Later on Piero secretly sold Leonardo's buckler to some merchants in Florence for a hundred ducats; and not long afterwards it came into the hands of the duke of Milan, who paid those merchants three hundred ducats for it.

Leonardo then painted a Madonna, a very fine work which came into the possession of Pope Clement VII; one of the details in this picture was a vase of water containing some flowers, painted with wonderful realism, which had on them dewdrops that looked more convincing than the real thing.

For his very close friend Antonio Segni, Leonardo drew on a sheet of paper a Neptune executed with such fine draughtsmanship and diligence that it was utterly convincing. In this picture could be seen the restless ocean and Neptune's chariot drawn by sea-horses, and the sprites, the sea-monsters, and the winds, along with some very beautiful heads of sea-gods. This was presented by Antonio's son Fabio to Giovanni Gaddi, with this epigram:

> *Pinxit Virgilius Neptunum, pinxit Homerus,*
> *Dum maris undisoni per vada flectit equos.*
> *Mente quidem vates illum conspexit uterque,*
> *Vincius ast oculis; jureque vincit eos.**

Leonardo then took it in mind to do a painting in oils showing the head of Medusa attired with a coil of serpents, the strangest and most extravagant invention imaginable. But this was a work that needed time, and so as with most of the things he did it was never finished. Today it is kept among the fine works of art in the palace of Duke Cosimo, along with the head of an angel raising one arm, which is foreshortened as it comes forward from the shoulder to the elbow, and lifting a hand to its breast with the other.

One of the remarkable aspects of Leonardo's talent was the extremes he went to, in his anxiety to achieve solidity of modelling, in the use of inky shadows. Thus to get the

---

* Virgil and Homer both have shown us Neptune guide
  His steeds amid the billows of the roaring main.
  These poets, though, have seen him but with mental gaze,
  Vinci with vision real; and 'tis truth to hail
  Vinci as victor.

darkest possible grounds Leonardo selected blacks that made deeper shadows and were indeed blacker than any other, endeavouring to make his lights all the brighter by contrast. However, he eventually succeeded so well that his paintings were wholly devoid of light and the subjects looked as if they were being seen by night rather than clearly defined by daylight. All this came from his striving to obtain ever more relief and to bring his art to absolute perfection. I must mention another habit of Leonardo's: he was always fascinated when he saw a man of striking appearance, with a strange head of hair or beard; and anyone who attracted him he would follow about all day long and end up seeing so clearly in his mind's eye that when he got home he could draw him as if he were standing there in the flesh. There are many drawings of both male and female heads which he did in this way, and I have several examples of them in the book of drawings mentioned so often before, such as the sketch of Amerigo Vespucci, which shows the head of a very handsome old man drawn in charcoal, or of Scaramuccia, the leader of the gipsies, which Giambullari subsequently left to Donato Valdambrini of Arezzo, canon of San Lorenzo.

Leonardo also started work on a panel picture showing the Adoration of the Magi and containing a number of beautiful details, especially the heads; this painting, however, which was in the house of Amerigo Benci, opposite the Loggia de' Peruzzi, like so many of his works remained unfinished.

Meanwhile in Milan, following the death of Duke Gian Galeazzo, Ludovico Sforza took over the state (in the year 1494) and did Leonardo the honour of inviting him to visit Milan so that he could hear him play the lyre, an instrument of which the new duke was very fond. Leonardo took with him a lyre that he had made himself, mostly of silver, in the shape of a horse's head (a very strange and novel design) so that the sound should be more sonorous and resonant. Leonardo's performance was therefore superior to that of all the other musicians who had come to Ludovico's court. Leonardo was also the most talented improviser in verse of his time. Moreover, he was a sparkling conversationalist, and after they had spoken together the duke developed almost boundless love and admiration for his talents. He begged Leonardo to paint for him an altarpiece containing a Nativity, which he then sent to the emperor.

Leonardo also executed in Milan, for the Dominicans of Santa Maria delle Grazie, a marvellous and beautiful painting of the Last Supper. Having depicted the heads of the apostles full of splendour and majesty, he deliberately left the head of Christ unfinished, convinced he would fail to give it the divine spirituality it demands. This all but finished work has ever since been held in the greatest veneration by the Milanese and others. In it Leonardo brilliantly succeeded in envisaging and reproducing the tormented anxiety of the apostles to know who had betrayed their master; so in their faces one can

11

read the emotions of love, dismay, and anger, or rather sorrow, at their failure to grasp the meaning of Christ. And this excites no less admiration than the contrasted spectacle of the obstinacy, hatred, and treachery in the face of Judas or, indeed, than the incredible diligence with which every detail of the work was executed. The texture of the very cloth on the table is counterfeited so cunningly that the linen itself could not look more realistic.

It is said that the prior used to keep pressing Leonardo, in the most importunate way, to hurry up and finish the work, because he was puzzled by Leonardo's habit of sometimes spending half a day at a time contemplating what he had done so far; if the prior had had his way, Leonardo would have toiled like one of the labourers hoeing in the garden and never put his brush down for a moment. Not satisfied with this, the prior then complained to the duke, making such a fuss that the duke was constrained to send for Leonardo and, very tactfully, question him about the painting, although he showed perfectly well that he was only doing so because of the prior's insistence. Leonardo, knowing he was dealing with a prince of acute and discerning intelligence, was willing (as he never had been with the prior) to explain his mind at length; and so he talked to the duke for a long time about the art of painting. He explained that men of genius sometimes accomplish most when they work the least; for, he added, they are thinking out inventions and forming in their minds the perfect ideas which they subsequently express and reproduce with their hands. Leonardo then said that he still had two heads to paint: the head of Christ was one, and for this he was unwilling to look for any human model, nor did he dare suppose that his imagination could conceive the beauty and divine grace that properly belonged to the incarnate Deity. Then, he said, he had yet to do the head of Judas, and this troubled him since he did not think he could imagine the features that would form the countenance of a man who, despite all the blessings he had been given, could so cruelly steel his will to betray his own master and the creator of the world. However, added Leonardo, he would try to find a model for Judas, and if he did not succeed in doing so, why then he was not without the head of that tactless and importunate prior. The duke roared with laughter at this and said that Leonardo had every reason in the world for saying so. The unfortunate prior retired in confusion to worry the labourers working in his garden, and he left off worrying Leonardo, who skilfully finished the head of Judas and made it seem the very embodiment of treachery and inhumanity. The head of Christ remained, as was said, unfinished.

This noble painting was so finely composed and executed that the King of France subsequently wanted to remove it to his kingdom. He tried all he could to find architects to make cross-stays of wood and iron with which the painting could be protected and brought safely to France, without any regard for expense, so great was his desire to have it. But as the painting was done on a wall his majesty failed to have his way and it remained in the possession of the Milanese. While he was working on the Last Supper, in the same refectory where there is a painting of the Passion done in the old manner, on the end wall, Leonardo portrayed Ludovico himself with his eldest son, Massimiliano; and on the other side, with the Duchess Beatrice, his other son Francesco, both of whom later became dukes of Milan; and all these figures are beautifully painted.

While he was engaged on this work Leonardo proposed to the duke that he should make a huge equestrian statue in bronze as a memorial to his father; then he started and carried the work forward on such a scale that it was impossible to finish it. There have even been some to say (men's opinions are so various and, often enough, so envious and spiteful) that Leonardo had no intention of finishing it when he started. This was because it was so large that it proved an insoluble problem to cast it in one piece; and one can realize why, the outcome being what it was, many came to the conclusion they did, seeing that so many of his works remained unfinished. The truth, however, is surely that Leonardo's profound and discerning mind was so ambitious that this was itself an impediment; and the reason he failed was because he endeavoured to add excellence to excellence and perfection to perfection. As our Petrarch has said, the desire outran the performance. In fact, those who saw the great clay model that Leonardo made considered that they had never seen a finer or more magnificent piece of work. It was preserved until the French came to Milan under King Louis and smashed it to pieces. Also lost is a little wax model which was held to be perfect, together with a reference book which Leonardo composed on the anatomy of horses. Leonardo then applied himself, even more assiduously, to the study of human anatomy, in which he collaborated with that excellent philosopher Marc Antonio della Torre, who was then lecturing at Pavia and who wrote on the subject. Della Torre, I have heard, was one of the first to illustrate the problems of medicine by the teachings of Galen and to throw true light on anatomy, which up to then had been obscured by the shadows of ignorance. In this he was wonderfully served by the intelligence, work, and hand of Leonardo, who composed a book annotated in pen and ink in which he did meticulous drawings in red chalk of bodies he had dissected himself. He showed all the bone structure, adding in order all the nerves and covering them with the muscles: the first attached to the skeleton, the second that hold it firm and the third that move it. In the various sections he wrote his observations in puzzling characters (written in reverse with the left hand) which cannot be deciphered by anyone who does not know the trick of reading them in a mirror.

Many of Leonardo's manuscripts on human anatomy are in the possession of Francesco Melzi, a Milanese gentleman who was a handsome boy when Leonardo was alive and who was greatly loved by him. Francesco cherishes and preserves these papers as relics of Leonardo, together with the portrait of that artist of such happy memory. Reading Leonardo's writings one is astonished at the brilliant way in which this inspired artist discussed so thoroughly art and anatomy (the muscles, nerves, and veins) and indeed every kind of subject. There are also some of his papers in the possession of a Milanese painter (again written in reverse with the left hand) which discuss painting and methods of drawing and colouring. Not long ago this man came to Florence to see me with the object of having the work printed, and later he went to Rome to put this into effect; but I do not know what happened then.

Anyhow, to return to Leonardo's works: when during his lifetime the king of France came to Milan, Leonardo was asked to devise some unusual entertainment, and so he constructed a lion which after walking a few steps opened its breast to reveal a cluster of lilies. It was in Milan that Leonardo took for his servant a Milanese called Salai, a very attractive youth of unusual grace and looks, with very beautiful hair which he wore curled in ringlets and which delighted his master. Leonardo taught Salai a great deal about painting, and some of the works in Milan which are attributed to him were retouched by Leonardo.

Then Leonardo went back to Florence where he found

that the Servite friars had commissioned Filippino to paint the altarpiece for the high altar of the Annunziata. Leonardo remarked that he would gladly have undertaken the work himself, and when he heard this, like the good-hearted person he was, Filippino decided to withdraw. Then the friars, to secure Leonardo's services, took him into their house and met all his expenses and those of his household. He kept them waiting a long time without even starting anything, and then finally he did a cartoon showing Our Lady with St Anne and the Infant Christ. This work not only won the astonished admiration of all the artists but when finished for two days it attracted to the room where it was exhibited a crowd of men and women, young and old, who flocked there, as if they were attending a great festival, to gaze in amazement at the marvels he had created. For in the face of Our Lady are seen all the simplicity and loveliness and grace that can be conferred on the mother of Christ, since Leonardo wanted to show the humility and the modesty appropriate to an image of the Virgin who is overflowing with joy at seeing the beauty of her Son. She is holding him tenderly on her lap, and she lets her pure gaze fall on St John, who is depicted as a little boy playing with a lamb; and this is not without a smile from St Anne, who is supremely joyful as she contemplates the divinity of her earthly progeny. These ideas were truly worthy of Leonardo's intellect and genius. As I shall describe, this cartoon was subsequently taken to France.

Leonardo also did a portrait of Ginevra, the wife of Amerigo Benci, a very beautiful painting. He abandoned the work he was doing for the friars and they went back to Filippino, who, however, died before he could finish it.

For Francesco del Giocondo Leonardo undertook to execute the portrait of his wife, Mona Lisa. He worked on this painting for four years, and then left it still unfinished; and today it is in the possession of King Francis of France, at Fontainebleau. If one wanted to see how faithfully art can imitate nature, one could readily perceive it from this head; for here Leonardo subtly reproduced every living detail. The eyes had their natural lustre and moistness, and around them were the lashes and all those rosy and pearly tints that demand the greatest delicacy of execution. The eyebrows were completely natural, growing thickly in one place and lightly in another and following the pores of the skin. The nose was finely painted, with rosy and delicate nostrils as in life. The mouth, joined to the flesh-tints of the face by the red of the lips, appeared to be living flesh rather than paint. On looking closely at the pit of her throat one could swear that the pulses were beating. Altogether this picture was painted in a manner to make the most confident artist – no matter who – despair and lose heart. Leonardo also made use of this device: while he was painting Mona Lisa, who was a very beautiful woman, he employed singers and musicians or jesters to keep her full of merriment and so chase away the melancholy that painters usually give to portraits. As a result, in this painting of Leonardo's there was a smile so pleasing that it seemed divine rather than human; and those who saw it were amazed to find that it was as alive as the original.

The great achievements of this inspired artist so increased his prestige that everyone who loved art, or rather every single person in Florence, was anxious for him to leave the city some memorial; and it was being proposed everywhere that Leonardo should be commissioned to do some great and notable work which would enable the state to be honoured and adorned by his discerning talent, grace, and judgement. As it happened the great hall of the council was being constructed under the architectural direction of Giuliano Sangallo, Simone Pollaiuolo (known as Cronaca), Michelangelo Buonarroti, and Baccio d'Agnolo, as I shall relate at greater length in the right place. It was finished in a hurry, and after the head of the government and the chief citizens had conferred together, it was publicly announced that a splendid painting would be commissioned from Leonardo. And then he was asked by Piero Soderini, the Gonfalonier of Justice, to do a decorative painting for the council hall. As a start, therefore, Leonardo began work in the Hall of the Pope, in Santa Maria Novella, on a cartoon illustrating an incident in the life of Niccolò Piccinino, a commander of Duke Filippo of Milan. He showed a group of horsemen fighting for a standard, in a drawing which was regarded as very fine and successful because of the wonderful ideas he expressed in his interpretation of the battle. In the drawing, rage, fury, and vindictiveness are displayed both by the men and by the horses, two of which with their forelegs interlocked are battling with their teeth no less fiercely than their riders are struggling for the standard, the staff of which has been grasped by a soldier who, as he turns and spurs his horse to flight, is trying by the strength of his shoulders to wrest it by force from the hands of four others. Two of them are struggling for it with one hand and attempting with the other to cut the staff with their raised swords; and an old soldier in a red cap roars out as he grips the staff with one hand and with the other raises a scimitar and aims a furious blow to cut off both the hands of those who are gnashing their teeth and ferociously defending their standard. Besides this, on the ground between the legs of the horses there are two figures, foreshortened, shown fighting together; the one on the ground has over him a soldier who has raised his arm as high as possible to plunge his dagger with greater force into the throat of his enemy, who struggles frantically with his arms and legs to escape death.

It is impossible to convey the fine draughtsmanship with which Leonardo depicted the soldiers' costumes, with their distinctive variations, or the helmet-crests and the other ornaments, not to speak of the incredible mastery that he displayed in the forms and lineaments of the horses which, with their bold spirit and muscles and shapely beauty, Leonardo portrayed better than any other artist. It is said that to draw the cartoon Leonardo constructed an ingenious scaffolding that he could raise or lower by drawing it together or extending it. He also conceived the wish to paint the picture in oils, but to do this he mixed such a thick composition for laying on the wall that, as he continued his painting in the hall, it started to run and spoil what had been done. So shortly afterwards he abandoned the work.

Leonardo was very proud and instinctively generous. According to one story, he once went along to the bank to draw his usual monthly salary from Piero Soderini and the cashier wanted to give him a few packets of pennies which he refused to take, saying that he was no 'penny painter'. As the painting had not been finished, he was accused of cheating Piero Soderini and there were murmurings against him. So Leonardo went round his friends and got the money together to repay Soderini; but Piero would not accept it.

Leonardo went to Rome with Duke Giuliano de' Medici on the election of Pope Leo who was a great student of natural philosophy, and especially of alchemy. And in Rome he experimented with a paste made out of a certain kind of wax and made some light and billowy figures in the form of animals which he inflated with his mouth as he walked along and which flew above the ground until all the air escaped. To the back of a very odd-looking lizard that was found by the gardener of the Belvedere he attached with a mixture of quicksilver some wings, made from the scales stripped from other lizards, which quivered as it walked along. Then, after he had given it eyes, horns, and a beard he tamed the creature, and keeping it in a box he used to show it to his friends and frighten the life out of them. Again, Leonardo used to get the intestines of a bullock scraped completely free of their fat, cleaned and made so fine that they could be compressed into the palm of one hand; then he would fix one end of them to a pair of bellows lying in another room, and when they were inflated they filled the room in which they were and forced anyone standing there into a corner. Thus he could expand this translucent and airy stuff to fill a large space after occupying only a little, and he compared it to genius. He perpetrated hundreds of follies of this kind, and he also experimented with mirrors and made the most outlandish experiments to discover oils for painting and varnish for preserving the finished works.

At that time for Baldassare Turini of Pescia, who was Pope Leo's datary, Leonardo executed with extraordinary diligence and skill a small picture of the Madonna and Child. But either because of the mistakes made by whoever primed the panel with gesso, or because of his own capricious way of mixing any number of grounds and colours, it is now spoilt. In another small picture he did the portrait of a little boy which is wonderfully beautiful and graceful. And both of these pictures are now in the possession of Giulio Turini at Pescia.

Once, when he was commissioned a work by the Pope, Leonardo is said to have started at once to distil oils and various plants in order to prepare the varnish; and the Pope is supposed to have exclaimed: 'Oh dear, this man will never do anything. Here he is thinking about finishing the work before he even starts it!'

Leonardo and Michelangelo strongly disliked each other, and so Michelangelo left Florence because of their rivalry (with permission from Duke Giuliano) after he had been summoned by the Pope to discuss the completion of the façade of San Lorenzo; and when he heard this Leonardo also left Florence and went to France. The king had obtained several of his works and was very devoted to him, and he asked Leonardo to paint the cartoon of St Anne. But, characteristically, Leonardo for a long time put him off with mere words.

Finally, in his old age Leonardo lay sick for several months, and feeling that he was near to death he earnestly resolved to learn about the doctrines of the Catholic faith and of the good and holy Christian religion. Then, lamenting bitterly, he confessed and repented, and, although he could not stand up, supported by his friends and servants he received the Blessed Sacrament from his bed. He was joined by the king, who often used to pay him affectionate visits, and having respectfully raised himself in his bed he told the king about his illness and what had caused it, and he protested that he had offended God and mankind by not working at his art as he should have done. Then he was seized by a paroxysm, the forerunner of death, and, to show him favour and to soothe his pain, the king held his head. Conscious of the great honour being done to him, the inspired Leonardo breathed his last in the arms of the king; he was then seventy-five years old.

All who had known Leonardo were grieved beyond words by their loss, for no one had ever shed such lustre on the art of painting.

In appearance he was striking and handsome, and his magnificent presence brought comfort to the most troubled soul; he was so persuasive that he could bend other people to his own will. He was physically so strong that he could withstand any violence; with his right hand he would bend the iron ring of a doorbell or a horseshoe as if they were lead. He was so generous that he sheltered and fed all his friends, rich or poor, provided they were of some talent or worth. By his every action Leonardo adorned and honoured the meanest and humblest dwelling-place. Through his birth, therefore, Florence received a very great gift, and through his death it sustained an incalculable loss. In painting he brought to the technique of colouring in oils a way of darkening the shadows which has enabled modern painters to give great vigour and relief to their figures. He showed his powers as a sculptor in the three bronze figures over the north door of San Giovanni which were executed by Giovanfrancesco Rustici, under Leonardo's direction, and which as far as design and finish are concerned are the finest casts yet seen in modern times.

Because of Leonardo we have a deeper knowledge of human anatomy and the anatomy of the horse. And because of his many wonderful gifts (although he accomplished far more in words than in deeds) his name and fame will never be extinguished. This was written in praise of Leonardo by Giovan Battista Strozzi:

> *Vince costui pur solo*
> *Tutti altri, e vince Fidia e vince Apelle,*
> *E tutto lor vittoriosi stuolo.**

One of Leonardo's pupils was Giovanni Antonio Boltraffio of Milan, a very skilful and discerning artist who in 1500 in the church of the Misericordia, outside Bologna, painted in oils a carefully finished picture of the Madonna and Child, St John the Baptist, and a nude St Sebastian, with a portrait of the donor kneeling in prayer. On this very beautiful panel he signed his name, adding that he was a pupil of Leonardo. He did other works at Milan and elsewhere, but it is enough to have described the best of them.

Another of Leonardo's pupils was Marco Uggioni, who in Santa Maria della Pace painted the Assumption of the Virgin and the Marriage of Cana in Galilee.

---

* Da Vinci vanquished alone all others, he vanquished Phidias and Apelles, and all their victorious followers.

Life of Fra Filippo Lippi

FLORENTINE PAINTER, *c*. 1406–69

Fra Filippo di Tommaso Lippi, a Carmelite, was born in Florence, in a street called Ardiglione, below the Canto alla Cucilia and behind the Carmelite Convent. The death of his father left him, at the age of two, a sad and solitary orphan, since his mother had died not long after he was born. He was put under the care of his aunt, Mona Lapaccia, Tommaso's sister, but she found it a struggle to bring him up and, when she could no longer manage, sent him, at the age of eight, to be a friar in the Carmelite Convent. At the convent he showed himself dexterous and ingenious in any work he had to do with his hands, but equally dull and incapable of learning when it came to his books; so he never spent any time studying his letters, which he regarded with great distaste. The boy (who was called by his secular name, Filippo) was placed with the other novices in the charge of the master teaching grammar to see what he could learn; but instead of studying he spent all his time scrawling pictures on his own books and those of others, and so eventually the prior decided to give him every chance and opportunity of learning to paint.

At that time the chapel of the Carmine had been freshly painted by Masaccio and its great beauty attracted Fra Filippo so much that he used to go every day in his spare time and practise in company with many other young artists who were always drawing there. He showed himself so superior to the rest in skill and knowledge that it was held for certain that one day he would do marvellous things; indeed, it was a miracle how many fine works he did produce before his maturity, while he was still in his salad days. Before very long he did a painting in *terra verde* in the cloister, near to Masaccio's *Consecration*, of a pope approving the Rule of the Carmelites, and he executed various frescoes on walls in many parts of the church, notably a St John the Baptist with some scenes from his life. His work improved every day and he came to understand Masaccio's style so well that his own pictures resembled those of Masaccio, and it was often said that Masaccio's soul had entered into his body. On a pilaster in the church, near the organ, he did a painting of St Marziale which bore comparison with Masaccio's work and which made his reputation. Then, in response to the praises he heard from all sides, at the age of seventeen he boldly threw off his friar's habit.

Now one day he happened to be enjoying himself with some of his friends in a little boat on the sea off the March of Ancona when they were all seized by the Moorish galleys that were scouring those parts, taken captive to Barbary, and put in chains. He stayed in this wretched condition for eighteen months. But one day when the opportunity presented itself he took it into his head to do a portrait of his master, with whom he was very familiar, and using a piece of dead coal from the fire he drew him on a white wall, full length in his Moorish costume. The other slaves reported this to his master, and since neither drawing nor painting were known in those parts everyone was astounded by what he had accomplished and he was, as a result, freed from the chains in which he had been kept so long. It was a glorious thing for the art of painting that it caused someone with the lawful authority to condemn and punish to do the opposite, giving his slave affection and liberty in the place of torture and death.

So, after he had done some painting in colour for his master, Fra Filippo was brought safely to Naples where for King Alfonso, then duke of Calabria, he painted a panel in tempera for the castle chapel, where the guardroom is now. He then determined to return to Florence, where he stayed for several months, executing a very beautiful altarpiece for the nuns of Sant' Ambrogio. This won him the affection of Cosimo de' Medici who became a close friend of his.

Fra Filippo also did a panel picture for the chapter-house of Santa Croce and another, which was placed in the chapel in the house of the Medici, showing the Nativity of Christ. As well as this, for the wife of Cosimo de' Medici he painted a panel picture of the Nativity of Christ with St John the Baptist, which was to be placed in the hermitage of Camaldoli in one of the hermits' cells dedicated to St John the Baptist which she had had built as an act of devotion. And he painted some little scenes that Cosimo sent as a gift to Pope Eugene IV, the Venetian. This work won Fra Filippo the favour of the Pope himself.

It is said that Fra Filippo was so lustful that he would give anything to enjoy a woman he wanted if he thought he could have his way; and if he couldn't buy what he wanted, then he would cool his passion by painting her portrait and reasoning with himself. His lust was so violent that when it took hold of him he could never concentrate on his work. And because of this, one time or other when he was doing something for Cosimo de' Medici in Cosimo's house, Cosimo had him locked in so that he wouldn't wander away and waste time. After he had been confined for a few days, Fra Filippo's amorous or rather his animal desires drove him one night to seize a pair of scissors, make a rope from his bed-sheets and escape through a window to pursue his own pleasures for days on end. When Cosimo discovered that he was gone, he searched for him and eventually got him back to work. And after that he always allowed him to come and go as he liked, having regretted the way he had shut him up before and realizing how dangerous it was for such a madman to be confined. Cosimo determined for the future to keep a hold on him by affection and kindness and, being served all the more readily, he used to say that artists of genius were to be treated with respect, not used as hacks.

For the church of Santa Maria Primerana, on the piazza at Fiesole, Fra Filippo did a panel picture of the Annunciation of Our Lady, finished with wonderful care, in which the figure of the angel is so beautiful that one can hardly doubt it has come from heaven. He did two panel pictures for the Murate, the convent of the enclosed Order of nuns: one for the high altar, showing the Annunciation, and the other over another altar in the same church containing scenes from the lives of SS. Benedict and Bernard. And in the palace of the Signoria he executed a panel picture of the Annunciation which is over one of the doors, and a painting of St Bernard which is over another. For the sacristy of Santo Spirito at Florence he did a panel picture showing Our Lady surrounded by angels and with saints on either side. This is an outstanding work which our leading artists have always held in reverence.

In the chapel of the wardens in San Lorenzo Fra Filippo painted a panel picture again showing the Annunciation, as well as another for the Della Stufa Chapel which was left unfinished. In Santi Apostoli at Florence, for one of the chapels, he painted a panel with various figures, grouped round Our Lady, and in Arezzo he was commissioned by Carlo Marsuppini to paint for the monks of Monte Oliveto the altarpiece for the chapel of St Bernard, showing the Coronation of Our Lady with a number of saints. When he painted this picture (which is still so fresh that it looks as if it has only just been finished) Fra Filippo was told by Carlo to pay special attention to the rendering of the hands, as his work had been adversely criticized in this respect. So from then onwards Filippo always covered the hands he painted with draperies or else used some other technique to escape censure. In this particular work he did a portrait of Carlo Marsuppini from life. Meanwhile, for the nuns of the Annalena at Florence he painted a panel picture showing Christ in the Manger; and there are also some paintings of his in Padua. To Cardinal Barbo at Rome he sent two small scenes with tiny figures which were skilfully executed and very carefully finished: it may be said here, in fact, that his paintings were always done with astonishing grace and finely composed and finished, and, consequently, he has always won the most lavish praise and respect from our artists, both living and dead. So long as his innumerable works are left undamaged by the ravages of time, their qualities will always command the highest respect.

In Prato near Florence, where he had some relations, Fra Filippo stayed for many months doing a great deal of work in various parts of the district in company with Fra Diamante of the Carmelite convent at Prato, who had been his companion when they were novices together. Subsequently, he was asked by the nuns to paint the altar-piece for the high altar of Santa Margherita, and it was when he was working at this that he one day caught sight of the daughter of Francesco Buti of Florence, who was living there as a novice or ward. Fra Filippo made advances to the girl, who was called Lucrezia and who was very beautiful and graceful, and he succeeded in persuading the nuns to let him use her as a model for the figure of Our Lady in his painting. This opportunity left him even more infatuated, and by various ways and means he managed to steal her from the nuns, taking her away on the very day that she was going to see the exposition of the Girdle of Our Lady, one of the great relics of Prato. This episode disgraced the nuns, and Francesco, the girl's father, never smiled again. He did all he could to get her back, but either from fear or some other reason she would never leave Fra Filippo; and by him she had a son, Filippo, who became, like his father, a famous and accomplished painter.

There are two of Fra Filippo's panel pictures in San Domenico of Prato; and a Madonna in the gallery of the church of San Francesco. It proved possible to move this painting from its original position to where it is now without damaging it by cutting away the wall and giving the section a wooden framework. There is also a little panel by Fra Filippo, over a well in the courtyard of the alms-house of Francesco di Marco, which contains the portrait of Francesco, who was the creator and founder of that pious foundation. And in the parish church at Prato there is a small panel of his, over the side door as one ascends the steps, showing the death of St Bernard, by the touch of whose bier many cripples are being restored to health. In this painting are a number of friars lamenting their dead master; and it is marvellous to see how skilfully and truthfully Fra Filippo has expressed grief and sadness in the attitudes of their heads. The draperies in this picture, namely, the friars' robes, are shown with a number of very beautiful folds, and their excellent design, colouring, and composition deserve every praise, as do the grace and proportion with which Fra Filippo delicately executed the whole work.

To have some memorial of him, the wardens of the parish church commissioned Fra Filippo to paint the chapel of the high altar; and he fully demonstrated his capabilities in the excellence and artistry of the work as a whole and, in particular, in its marvellous draperies and heads. In these frescoes Fra Filippo made his figures larger than life, thus showing the way to modern artists to achieve the grandeur of the style of our own day. They contain also various figures dressed in clothes which were not contemporary, and by this departure Fra Filippo prompted the artists of that time to abandon the kind of simplicity which, far from reflecting the style of the ancient world, was simply old-fashioned. The work includes scenes from the life of St Stephen, the patron saint of the church, covering the right-hand wall, namely, the Disputation, the Stoning, and the Death of the first martyr. Fra Filippo showed such zeal and fervour in

St Stephen's face as he disputes with the Jews that it is difficult to imagine let alone to describe; and this is to say nothing of the contempt and hatred, and the anger at being vanquished, expressed in the faces and the various attitudes of those Jews. He depicted even more convincingly the fury and brutality of St Stephen's executioners, who are seizing stones of all sizes, with a fearsome grinding of teeth and with cruel and outrageous gestures. Yet St Stephen stands serene before this terrible onslaught, his face lifted towards heaven, praying with great charity and fervour to the Eternal Father for the very men who are murdering him. These concepts are all extremely fine, and they show other painters how important it is to be able to express new ideas and to convey the emotions. Fra Filippo was so expert in this respect that one cannot look at the grief-stricken attitudes of those burying St Stephen and the sad and afflicted expressions of some of the mourners without being deeply moved.

On the other side of the chapel he painted scenes from the life of John the Baptist: the Nativity, the Preaching in the Wilderness, the Baptism, the Feast of Herod, and the Beheading. The light of divine inspiration shines from the face of the preacher and the various gestures of the crowd express the joy and sorrow of the men and women held and absorbed by the ministrations of St John. Beauty and goodness are apparent in the Baptism scene; and in the picture of Herod's banquet we see depicted all the sumptuousness of this occasion, along with the skill of

Herodias, the stupor of the guests and the horrified consternation caused when the head is offered on a charger. About the table Fra Filippo painted a great many figures, in very expressive poses, with beautifully executed draperies and expressions. Among them he included a portrait of himself, drawn with a mirror, clothed in the black habit of a priest; and in the scene showing the mourning for St Stephen he showed his pupil, Fra Diamante. (This work was certainly his best for the reasons I have already given and also because in it he made the figures somewhat larger than life; and this prompted those who came after him to paint with more grandeur. Fra Filippo was so highly regarded for his good qualities and his virtuosity that the many blameworthy circumstances in his life were passed over in silence.) He also portrayed in the work I have been discussing Cosimo de' Medici's natural son, Carlo, at that time the provost of the church, which received many benefactions from him and his family.

After he had finished these frescoes, Fra Filippo, in 1463, painted a panel in tempera for the church of San Jacopo at Pistoia, containing a very beautiful Annunciation, with a lively portrait of Jacopo Bellucci, who commissioned the work. In the house of Pulidoro Bracciolini there is a picture by Fra Filippo of the Birth of Our Lady; and for the hall of the Tribunal of the Eight at Florence he painted in tempera a Madonna and Child on a lunette. There is a very beautiful Madonna from his hand in the house of Lodovico Capponi; and in the possession of Bernardo Vecchietti, a Florentine gentleman of outstanding accomplishment and merit, is a beautiful little picture of his, showing St Augustine at his studies. Finer still is the St Jerome in Penitence, a picture of the same size which is in Duke Cosimo's wardrobe.

All Fra Filippo's work was outstanding, but in his smaller paintings he excelled even himself, producing pictures of incomparable grace and beauty, as we can see in all the predellas he did for his panels. His stature as a painter was such that none of his contemporaries and few modern painters have surpassed him. Michelangelo himself has always sung his praises and in many particulars has even imitated him. One of the paintings Fra Filippo did was for the church of San Domenico Vecchio at Perugia, a panel (subsequently placed on the high altar) containing a Madonna, St Peter, St Paul, St Louis, and St Anthony Abbot. And Alessandro degli Alessandri, a knight of that time and a friend of Fra Filippo's, commissioned from him, for the church of his villa at Vincigliata on the hillside of Fiesole, a panel depicting St Lawrence and other saints, among whom he painted Alessandro and two sons of his.

Fra Filippo liked to have cheerful people as his friends and himself lived a very merry life. He taught the art of painting to Fra Diamante, who executed many pictures for the Carmine at Prato and by imitating his master's style very closely achieved the highest perfection. Among those who studied with Fra Filippo in their youth were Sandro Botticelli, Pesellino, and Jacopo del Sellaio of Florence, who painted two panel pictures for San Frediano and one for the Carmine, in tempera. There were countless other artists to whom he affectionately taught the art of painting. He lived honourably from his work and he spent extravagantly on his love affairs, which he pursued all his life until the day he died.

Through the mediation of Cosimo de' Medici, Fra Filippo was asked by the commune of Spoleto to decorate the chapel in their principal church, dedicated to Our Lady. Working with Fra Diamante he made excellent progress, but he died before he could finish: they say that in one of those sublime love affairs he was always having the relations of the woman concerned had him poisoned. At any rate, Fra Filippo ended this life at the age of fifty-seven in the year 1438.

In his will he left his son Filippo, who was then ten years old, to the care of Fra Diamante, who brought the boy back to Florence and taught him the art of painting. On his return to Florence Fra Diamante took with him three hundred ducats that were owing from the commune, giving some of them to the boy and using the rest to buy things for himself. Filippo was placed with Sandro Botticelli, who was then regarded as a first-rate artist; and Fra Filippo himself was buried in a tomb of red-and-white marble erected by the people of Spoleto in the church he had painted.

Fra Filippo's death deeply grieved his many friends, especially Cosimo de' Medici and Pope Eugene. When he was alive the Pope wanted to give him a dispensation so that he could make Lucrezia, Francesco Buti's daughter, his legitimate wife; but as he wanted to stay free and give full rein to his desires Fra Filippo refused the offer. During the lifetime of Sixtus IV, Lorenzo de' Medici, who had been made an ambassador of Florence, went to Spoleto to ask the citizens for permission to remove Fra Filippo's body to Santa Maria del Fiore at Florence; but they told him that Spoleto lacked any great marks of distinction and especially the adornment of eminent men; and so they asked him as a favour to allow them to keep Filippo's body to honour Spoleto, adding that Florence had countless famous citizens, almost a superfluity, and so it could do without this one. So Lorenzo failed to get what he wanted. However, subsequently he determined to pay him the greatest honour he could, and be sent his son, Filippino, to Rome to decorate a chapel in his father's memory for the cardinal of Naples. On his way through Spoleto, Filippino was commissioned by Lorenzo to construct a marble tomb under the organ over the sacristy; and on this he spent a hundred gold ducats which were paid by Nofri Tornabuoni, director of the Medici Bank. He obtained from Angelo Politian the following epigram, which was carved on the tomb in antique letters:

Conditus hic ego sum picturae fama Philippus,
  Nulli ignota meae est gratia mira manus.
Artifices potuit digitis animare colores,
  Sperataque animos fallere voce diu.
Ipsa meis stupuit natura expressa figuris,
  Meque suis fassa est artibus esse parem.
Marmoreo tumolo Medices Laurentius hic me
  Condidit, ante humili pulvere tectus eram.*

Fra Filippo was a first-rate draughtsman, as can be seen in our book of drawings by the most famous painters, notably in some sheets containing his design for the picture of Santo Spirito and others showing the chapel of Prato.

---

* Here in this place do I, Filippo, rest
  Enshrin'd in token of my art's renown.
  All know the wondrous beauty of my skill;
  My touch gave life to lifeless paint, and long
  Deceiv'd the mind to think the forms would speak.
  Nature herself, as I reveal'd her, own'd
  In wonderment that I could match her arts.
  Beneath the lowly soil was I interr'd
  Ere this; but now Lorenzo Medici
  Hath laid me here within this marble tomb.

Life of Sandro Botticelli

In the time of the elder Lorenzo de' Medici, Lorenzo the
Magnificent, truly a golden age for men of talent, there
flourished an artist called Alessandro (which we shorten
to Sandro), whose second name, for reasons we shall see
later, was Botticelli. He was the son of a Florentine, Mariano Filipepi, who brought him up very conscientiously
and had him instructed in all those things usually taught
to young children before they are apprenticed. However,
although he easily mastered all that he wanted to, the boy
refused to settle down or be satisfied with reading, writing, and arithmetic; and finally, exasperated by his son's
restless mind, his father apprenticed him as a goldsmith
to a close companion of his own called Botticelli, who was
a very competent craftsman. Now at that time there was
a very close connexion – almost a constant intercourse –
between the goldsmiths and the painters, and so Sandro,
who was a very agile-minded young man and who had
already become absorbed by the arts of design, became
entranced by painting and determined to devote himself

to it. He told his father about his ambition, and Mariano, seeing the way his mind was inclined, took him to Fra Filippo of the Carmine, a great painter of that time, and, as Sandro himself wished, placed him with Fra Filippo to study painting.

Botticelli threw all his energies into his work, following and imitating his master so well that Fra Filippo grew very fond of him and taught him to such good effect that very soon his skill was greater than anyone would have anticipated. While still a young man Botticelli painted in the Mercanzia of Florence, among the pictures of virtues executed by Antonio and Piero Pollaiuolo, a figure representing Fortitude. In Santo Spirito in Florence, for the Bardi Chapel, he did a panel picture, very carefully painted and beautifully finished, with some olive trees and palms depicted with loving care. He also painted a panel picture for the Convertite Convent and another for the nuns of Santa Barnaba. In the church of Ognissanti, in the gallery by the door leading to the choir, he painted for the Vespucci family a fresco of St Augustine, over which he took very great pains in an attempt to surpass all his contemporaries but especially Domenico Ghirlandaio, who had painted a St Jerome on the other side. This work was very favourably received, for Botticelli succeeded in expressing in the head of the saint that air of profound meditation and subtle perception characteristic of men of wisdom who ponder continuously on difficult and elevated matters. As I said in my *Life* of Ghirlandaio, this year (1564) this painting of Botticelli's was removed safe and sound from its original position.

Because of the credit and reputation he acquired through his St Augustine, Botticelli was commissioned by the Guild of Porta Santa Maria to do a panel picture for San Marco showing the Coronation of Our Lady surrounded by a choir of angels, which he designed and executed very competently. He also carried out many works in the house of the Medici for Lorenzo the Magnificent, notably a life-size Pallas on a shield wreathed with fiery branches, and a St Sebastian. And in Santa Maria Maggiore at Florence, beside the chapel of the Panciatichi, there is a very beautiful Pietà with little figures.

For various houses in Florence Botticelli painted a number of round pictures, including many female nudes, of which there are still two extant at Castello, Duke Cosimo's villa, one showing the Birth of Venus, with her Cupids, being wafted to land by the winds and zephyrs, and the other Venus as a symbol of spring, being adorned with flowers by the Graces; all this work was executed with exquisite grace. In the Via de' Servi around a room in Giovanni Vespucci's house (which now belongs to Piero Salviati) Botticelli painted several pictures showing many beautiful and very vivacious figures, which were enclosed in walnut panelling and ornamentation. In the house of the Pucci he illustrated – with various little figures in four paintings of considerable charm and beauty – Boccaccio's story about Nastagio degli Onesto, and he also did a circular picture of the Epiphany. For a chapel belonging to the monks of Cestello he did a panel picture of the Annunciation. Then for San Piero Maggiore, by the side door, he did a panel for Matteo Palmieri, with a vast number of figures, showing the Assumption of Our Lady and the circles of heaven, the patriarchs, prophets and apostles, the evangelists, martyrs, confessors, doctors, virgins, and the hierarchy of angels, all taken from a drawing given to him by Matteo, a very learned and talented man. Botticelli painted this work with exquisite care and assurance, introducing the portraits of Matteo and his wife kneeling at the foot. Although the painting is so great that it should have silenced envy, it provoked some malevolent critics to allege, not being able to fault it on any other score, that both Matteo and Sandro had fallen into the sin of heresy. Whether this was so or not I am not the one to say; it is enough for me that the figures which Sandro painted in this picture are admirable for the care lavished on them, and the manner in which he has shown the circles of the heavens, introducing foreshortenings and intervals between his variously composed groups of angels and other figures, and executing the whole work with a fine sense of design.

At that time Sandro was commissioned to paint a small panel, with figures a foot and a half in length, which was placed in Santa Maria Novella between two doors in the principal façade on the left as one goes in by the centre door. The subject is the Adoration of the Magi, and the picture is remarkable for the emotion shown by the elderly man as he kisses the foot of Our Lord with wonderful tenderness and conveys his sense of relief at having come to the end of his long journey. This figure, the first of the kings, is a portrait of the elder Cosimo de' Medici, and it is the most convincing and natural of all the surviving portraits. The second king (a portrait of Giuliano de' Medici, the father of Pope Clement VII) is shown doing reverence with utterly absorbed devotion as he offers his gift to the Child. The third, also on his knees, is shown gratefully adoring the Child whom he acknowledges as the true Messiah; and this is Cosimo's son, Giovanni. The beauty of the heads that Sandro painted in this picture defies description: they are shown in various poses, some full-face, some in profile, some in three-quarters, some looking down, with a great variety of expressions and attitudes in the figures of young and old, and with all those imaginative details that demonstrate the artist's complete mastery of his craft. For Botticelli clearly distinguished the retinues belonging to each of the three kings, producing in the completed work a marvellous painting which today amazes every artist by its colouring, its design, and its composition.

His Adoration of the Magi made Botticelli so famous, both in Florence and elsewhere, that Pope Sixtus IV, having finished the building of the chapel for his palace at

Rome and wanting to have it painted, decided that he should be put in charge of the work. So Botticelli himself painted the following scenes for the chapel: Christ tempted by the devil; Moses slaying the Egyptian and accepting drink from the daughters of Jethro the Midianite; fire falling from heaven on the sacrifice of the sons of Aaron; and several portraits of canonized Popes in the niches above. Having won even greater fame and reputation among the many competitors who worked with him, artists from Florence and elsewhere, Botticelli was generously paid by the Pope; but living in his usual haphazard fashion he spent and squandered all he earned during his stay in Rome. Then, when he had finished and unveiled the work he had been commissioned, he immediately returned to Florence where, being a man of inquiring mind, he completed and printed a commentary on a part of Dante, illustrating the *Inferno*. He wasted a great deal of time on this, neglecting his work and thoroughly disrupting his life. He also printed many of his other drawings, but the results were inferior because the plates were badly engraved; the best was the Triumph of the Faith of Fra Girolamo Savonarola of Ferrara. Botticelli was a follower of Savonarola's, and this was why he gave up painting and then fell into considerable distress as he had no other source of income. None the less, he remained an obstinate member of the sect, becoming one of the *piagnoni*, the snivellers, as they were called then, and abandoning his work; so finally, as an old man, he found himself so poor that if Lorenzo de' Medici (for whom he had among other things done some work at the little hospital at Volterra) and then his friends and other worthy men who loved him for his talent had not come to his assistance, he would have almost died of hunger.

One of Sandro's paintings, a very highly regarded work to be found in San Francesco outside the Porta a San Miniato, is a Madonna in a circular picture with some angels, all lifesize.

He was a very good-humoured man and much given to playing jokes on his pupils and friends. For example, the story goes that one of his pupils, called Biagio, painted a circular picture exactly like the one of Botticelli's mentioned above, and that Sandro sold it for him to one of the citizens for six gold florins; then he found Biagio and told him:

'I've finally sold this picture of yours. So now you must hang it up high this evening so that it looks better, and then tomorrow morning go along and find the man who bought it so that you can show it to him properly displayed in a good light, and then he'll give you your money.'

'Oh, you've done marvellously,' said Biagio, who then went along to the shop, hung his picture at a good height, and left. In the meantime, Sandro and another of his pupils, Jacopo, had made several paper hats (like the ones the citizens wore) which they stuck with white wax over the heads of the eight angels that surrounded the

Madonna in his picture. Then, when the morning came, Biagio arrived with the citizen who had bought the painting (and who had been let into the joke). They went into the shop, where Biagio looked up and saw his Madonna seated not in the midst of angels but in the middle of the councillors of Florence, all wearing their paper hats! He was just about to roar out in anger and make excuses when he noticed that the man he was with had said nothing at all, and was in fact starting to praise the picture . . . so Biagio kept quiet himself. And at length he went home with him and was given his six florins, as the price agreed by Botticelli. Then he went back to the shop, a moment or two after Sandro and Jacopo had removed those paper hats, and he found that the angels he had painted were angels after all and was so stupefied that he was at a loss for words. Eventually he turned to Sandro and said:

'Sir, I don't know if I'm dreaming or if this is reality, but when I was here earlier those angels were wearing red hats, and now they're not. What's the meaning of it?'

'You've taken leave of your senses,' said Sandro. 'All that money has gone to your head. If what you say were true, do you think he'd have bought your picture?'

'That's so,' said Biagio, 'He didn't say a word. But all the same it struck me as very strange.'

Then all the other apprentices flocked round him and convinced him that he had had some kind of giddy spell.

Another time, a cloth-weaver moved into the house next to Sandro's and set up no less than eight looms which when they were working not only deafened poor Sandro with the noise of the treadles and the movement of the frames but also shook his whole house, the walls of which were no stronger than they should be. What with one thing and the other, he couldn't work or even stay in the house. Several times he begged his neighbour to do something about the nuisance, but the weaver retorted that in his own home he could and would do just what he liked. Finally, Sandro grew very angry, and on top of his roof, which was higher than his neighbour's and not all that substantial, he balanced an enormous stone (big enough to fill a wagon) which threatened to fall at the least movement of the wall and wreck the man's roof, ceilings, floors, and looms. Terrified at the prospect the cloth-weaver ran to Sandro only to be told, in his own words, that in his own house Botticelli could and would do just what he wanted to. So there being nothing else for it the man was obliged to come to reasonable terms and make himself a good neighbour.

According to another anecdote, for a joke Sandro once denounced one of his friends to the vicar as a heretic. The man appeared and demanded to know who had accused him and of what. When he was told that his accuser was Sandro, who had alleged that he believed with the Epicureans that the soul dies with the body, he demanded to see him before the judge. And when Sandro appeared on the scene, he said:

'Certainly that is what I believe as far as this man is

concerned, seeing that he's a brute. But apart from that, isn't it he who is the heretic, since although he scarcely knows how to read and write he did a commentary on Dante and took his name in vain?'

It is also said of Sandro that he was extraordinarily fond of any serious student of painting, and that he earned a great deal of money but wasted it all through carelessness and lack of management. Anyhow, after he had grown old and useless, unable to stand upright and moving about with the help of crutches, he died, ill and decrepit, at the age of seventy-eight, and he was buried in Ognissanti in Florence.

In Duke Cosimo's wardrobe there are two very beautiful female heads in profile by Botticelli, one of which is said to be the mistress of Lorenzo's brother, Giuliano de' Medici, and the other, Madonna Lucrezia de' Tornabuoni, Lorenzo's wife. In the same place there is a Bacchus of Sandro's, a very graceful figure shown raising a cask with both hands and putting it to its lips. In the Duomo at Pisa, in the chapel of the Impagliata, he started an Assumption with a choir of angels, but it displeased him and he left it unfinished. In San Francesco at Montevarchi he did the panel for the high altar, and he also did two angels for the parish church at Empoli, on the same side as Rossellino's St Sebastian.

Botticelli was one of the first to find out how to make standards and other draperies by plaiting the material so that the colours show on both sides without running.

That was how he made the baldachin of Orsanmichele, full of Madonnas, all different and all beautiful. It is clear that this method of treating the cloth preserves the work better than the use of acids, which eat the material away, even though because of its relative cheapness the latter is nowadays the more usual technique.

Sandro was an uncommonly good draughtsman and, in consequence, for some time after his death artists used to search out his drawings, and I have some of them in my book which show great skill and judgement. In the scenes he did he made a lavish use of figures, as can be seen in the decorative work he designed for the frieze of the processional cross of the friars of Santa Maria Novella.

Altogether, Sandra Botticelli's pictures merited the highest praise; he threw himself into his work with diligence and enthusiasm, as can be seen in the Adoration of the Magi in Santa Maria Novella, which I described earlier and which is a marvellous painting. Also very fine is the small circular picture by Sandro that can be seen in the prior's room in the Angeli at Florence, the figures being tiny but very graceful and beautifully composed. A Florentine gentleman, Fabio Segni, has in his possession a painting of the same size as the panel picture of the Magi; the subject is Apelles' Calumny. He himself gave this unimaginably beautiful painting to his close friend, Antonio Segni, and underneath it can be read these lines by Fabio:

Iudicio quemquam ne falso laedere tentent
Terrarum reges, parva tabella monet.
Huic similem Aegypti regi donavit Apelles;
Rex fuit et dignus munere, munus eo.*

* This little picture warns the rulers of the earth
  To shun the tyranny of judgement false.
  Apelles gave its like to Egypt's king; that king
  Was worthy of the gift, and it of him.

1. BOCCACCIO · *Mrs Rosie and the Priest*
2. GERARD MANLEY HOPKINS · *As kingfishers catch fire*
3. *The Saga of Gunnlaug Serpent-tongue*
4. THOMAS DE QUINCEY · *On Murder Considered as One of the Fine Arts*
5. FRIEDRICH NIETZSCHE · *Aphorisms on Love and Hate*
6. JOHN RUSKIN · *Traffic*
7. PU SONGLING · *Wailing Ghosts*
8. JONATHAN SWIFT · *A Modest Proposal*
9. *Three Tang Dynasty Poets*
10. WALT WHITMAN · *On the Beach at Night Alone*
11. KENKŌ · *A Cup of Sake Beneath the Cherry Trees*
12. BALTASAR GRACIÁN · *How to Use Your Enemies*
13. JOHN KEATS · *The Eve of St Agnes*
14. THOMAS HARDY · *Woman much missed*
15. GUY DE MAUPASSANT · *Femme Fatale*
16. MARCO POLO · *Travels in the Land of Serpents and Pearls*
17. SUETONIUS · *Caligula*
18. APOLLONIUS OF RHODES · *Jason and Medea*
19. ROBERT LOUIS STEVENSON · *Olalla*
20. KARL MARX AND FRIEDRICH ENGELS · *The Communist Manifesto*
21. PETRONIUS · *Trimalchio's Feast*
22. JOHANN PETER HEBEL · *How a Ghastly Story Was Brought to Light by a Common or Garden Butcher's Dog*
23. HANS CHRISTIAN ANDERSEN · *The Tinder Box*
24. RUDYARD KIPLING · *The Gate of the Hundred Sorrows*
25. DANTE · *Circles of Hell*
26. HENRY MAYHEW · *Of Street Piemen*
27. HAFEZ · *The nightingales are drunk*
28. GEOFFREY CHAUCER · *The Wife of Bath*
29. MICHEL DE MONTAIGNE · *How We Weep and Laugh at the Same Thing*
30. THOMAS NASHE · *The Terrors of the Night*
31. EDGAR ALLAN POE · *The Tell-Tale Heart*
32. MARY KINGSLEY · *A Hippo Banquet*
33. JANE AUSTEN · *The Beautifull Cassandra*
34. ANTON CHEKHOV · *Gooseberries*
35. SAMUEL TAYLOR COLERIDGE · *Well, they are gone, and here must I remain*
36. JOHANN WOLFGANG VON GOETHE · *Sketchy, Doubtful, Incomplete Jottings*
37. CHARLES DICKENS · *The Great Winglebury Duel*
38. HERMAN MELVILLE · *The Maldive Shark*
39. ELIZABETH GASKELL · *The Old Nurse's Story*
40. NIKOLAY LESKOV · *The Steel Flea*

41. HONORÉ DE BALZAC · *The Atheist's Mass*
42. CHARLOTTE PERKINS GILMAN · *The Yellow Wall-Paper*
43. C.P. CAVAFY · *Remember, Body . . .*
44. FYODOR DOSTOEVSKY · *The Meek One*
45. GUSTAVE FLAUBERT · *A Simple Heart*
46. NIKOLAI GOGOL · *The Nose*
47. SAMUEL PEPYS · *The Great Fire of London*
48. EDITH WHARTON · *The Reckoning*
49. HENRY JAMES · *The Figure in the Carpet*
50. WILFRED OWEN · *Anthem For Doomed Youth*
51. WOLFGANG AMADEUS MOZART · *My Dearest Father*
52. PLATO · *Socrates' Defence*
53. CHRISTINA ROSSETTI · *Goblin Market*
54. *Sindbad the Sailor*
55. SOPHOCLES · *Antigone*
56. RYŪNOSUKE AKUTAGAWA · *The Life of a Stupid Man*
57. LEO TOLSTOY · *How Much Land Does A Man Need?*
58. GIORGIO VASARI · *Leonardo da Vinci*
59. OSCAR WILDE · *Lord Arthur Savile's Crime*
60. SHEN FU · *The Old Man of the Moon*
61. AESOP · *The Dolphins, the Whales and the Gudgeon*
62. MATSUO BASHŌ · *Lips too Chilled*
63. EMILY BRONTË · *The Night is Darkening Round Me*
64. JOSEPH CONRAD · *To-morrow*
65. RICHARD HAKLUYT · *The Voyage of Sir Francis Drake Around the Whole Globe*
66. KATE CHOPIN · *A Pair of Silk Stockings*
67. CHARLES DARWIN · *It was snowing butterflies*
68. BROTHERS GRIMM · *The Robber Bridegroom*
69. CATULLUS · *I Hate and I Love*
70. HOMER · *Circe and the Cyclops*
71. D. H. LAWRENCE · *Il Duro*
72. KATHERINE MANSFIELD · *Miss Brill*
73. OVID · *The Fall of Icarus*
74. SAPPHO · *Come Close*
75. IVAN TURGENEV · *Kasyan from the Beautiful Lands*
76. VIRGIL · *O Cruel Alexis*
77. H. G. WELLS · *A Slip under the Microscope*
78. HERODOTUS · *The Madness of Cambyses*
79. *Speaking of Siva*
80. *The Dhammapada*